MLB (MAJ

(A Fascinating Book Containing Baseball Facts, Trivia, Images & Memory Recall Quiz: Suitable for Adults & Children)

By

Matthew Harper

Image Courtesy of laobc

Hi and a very warm welcome to "MLB (Major League Baseball)".

I'm one of those people who loves to hear about extraordinary facts or trivia about anything. They seem to be one of the few things my memory can actually recall. I'm not sure if it's to do with the shock or the "WoW" factor but for some reason my brain seems to store at least some of it for a later date.

I've always been a great believer in that whatever the subject, if a good teacher can inspire you and hold your attention, then you'll learn! Now I'm not a teacher but the system I've used in previous publications on Amazon seems to work well, particularly with children.

This edition includes a selection of those "WoW" facts combined with some pretty awesome pictures, if I say so myself! At the end there is a short "True or False" quiz to check memory recall and to help cement some of the information included in the book. Don't worry though, it's a bit of fun but at the same time, it helps to check your understanding.

Please note that if you're an expert on this subject then you may not find anything new here. If however you enjoy hearing sensational and extraordinary trivia and you like looking at some great pictures then I think you'll love it.

Matt.

I thought that before we get down to some of those amazing baseball facts, we might begin with some snapshots, just to get the juices flowing……….

HONUS WAGNER

MICKEY MANTLE

STAN MUSIAL

ROGER CLEMENS

Image Courtesy of Keith Allison

TY COBB

HANK AARON

Image Courtesy of Chris Evans

TED WILLIAMS

BARRY BONDS

WILLIE MAYS

BABE RUTH

Okay, that's it for the warm up; let's get on with the game......

Image Courtesy of tawm1972

Did you know that on 17th August 1957, Richie Ashburn of the Philadelphia Phillies hit a foul ball and managed to break the nose of Alice Roth (spectator)? Whilst she was being carried away on a stretcher, Richie hit another foul ball which again struck poor Alice, this time breaking a bone in her knee!

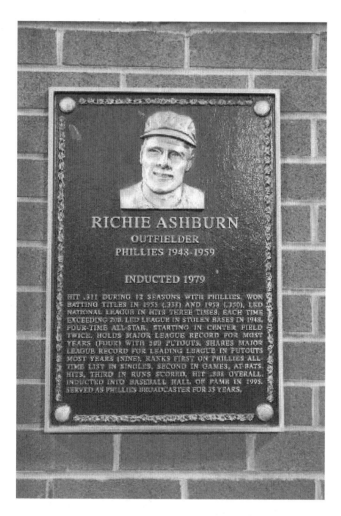

Image Courtesy of Peter Bond

Did you know that the first World Series was played in 1903? The Boston Americans won the series beating the Pittsburgh Pirates 5-3.

Did you know that Jim Abbott, (born 19/9/1967), was a former MLB pitcher despite being born without a right hand?

John Traub / Albuquerque Isotopes Baseball Club

Did you know that during World War II, the U.S. Army developed the BEANO T-13 hand grenade? The idea was that the spherical shape, size and weight of the grenade should emulate that of a baseball making it easier for American soldiers to throw the device further and with greater accuracy.

Image Courtesy of www.citysubwaycreatures.com

Did you know that each baseball game has 12,386,344 possible plays?

Image Courtesy of Herkie

Did you know that Raymond Johnson Chapman (Cleveland) is the only MLB player to have died during a major league baseball game? On the 16th August 1920, Chapman was struck in the head by a pitch from Carl Mays (Yankees pitcher). Hhe died the next day.

Image Courtesy of Jtesla16

Did you know that Jon Erich Rauch (pitcher) is the tallest player in MLB history with a height of 6 feet 11 inches (2.11 m)?

Image Courtesy of dbking

Did you also know that Eddie Gaedel, (8/6/1925 - 18/6/1961), was the shortest player in MLB history standing only 3 feet 7 inches tall (1.092 m)?

Image Courtesy of Dave Hogg

Did you know that under the rules, MLB umpires have to wear black underwear in case they happen to split their pants?

Image Courtesy of Keith Allison

Did you know that the lowest attendance recorded to date for an MLB game is 347? Largely due to Hurricane Irene in 2011, the Florida Marlins v the Cincinnati Reds broke the previous record of 653.

Image Courtesy of miamism

Did you know that a regulation baseball has 108 stitches?

Image Courtesy of JML78

Did you know that when Jimmy Pearsall hit his 100th home run in 1963, he ran around all the bases in the correct order but was facing backwards when he did it?

Did you know that Moisés Alou & Jorge Posada both urinate on their hands to make them tougher and to help improve their grips? Yuk!

Jorge Posada - Image Courtesy of Keith Allison

Did you know that in 1961, Bill Veeck, who had a controlling interest in the Chicago White Sox at that time, decided to hire dwarfs and midgets as vendors so as not to spoil the fans' view of the game?

Did you know that Robert Redford was accepted at the University of Colorado on a baseball scholarship?

Did you know that Roger Philip Bresnahan, American player and manager in MLB, introduced shin guards in 1907 and helped develop the first batting helmet?

Did you know that Ralph Kiner is the only player to date that has led the league in home runs for 7 years in a row?

Image Courtesy of slgckgc

Did you know that the MLB National League started in 1876 making it the oldest professional sports league still in existence?

Did you know that in 1977, Michael Jack Schmidt was the first player in baseball to earn a salary of $500,000?

Image Courtesy of Squelle

Did you know that since the 1950's, every single MLB baseball is rubbed in "Lena Blackburne Baseball Rubbing Mud"? This unique and extremely fine mud is said to originate from the New Jersey side of the Delaware River although the exact location is a closely guarded secret.

Image Courtesy of www.state.nj.us

Did you know that David Mark Winfield, (Baseball Hall of Fame), killed a seagull after throwing a ball whilst warming up before the fifth inning of a game in 1983? He was arrested and charged with cruelty to animals although the charges were dropped the very next day.

Did you know that Nolan Ryan, nicknamed "The Ryan Express", had more strikeouts in his career of 27 seasons than any other pitcher?

Did you know that to date, Cal Hubbard is the only person you will find in both the Pro-Football Hall of Fame & the Baseball Hall of Fame?

Did you know that Johnny Lee Bench, former baseball catcher & member of the National Baseball Hall of Fame, could hold 7 baseballs in one hand?

Source:
www.uc.edu/news/view.asp?infoID=1915&photo=image3

Did you know that Alex Rodriguez, nicknamed "A-Rod", is currently the youngest player ever to have hit more than 500 career home runs?

Image Courtesy of Keith Allison

Did you know that on June 9, 1999, manager Bobby Valentine of the New York Mets was ejected from a game against the Toronto Blue Jays, for arguing a call, by home-plate umpire Randy Marsh? Bobby returned an inning later wearing regular clothes and a fake moustache as a disguise. MLB fined him $5,000 & suspended him for 2 games for returning to a game after an ejection!

Image Courtesy of Keith Allison

Did you know that in 1976, the National Beep Baseball Association was created for visually impaired adults to play baseball? The organization promotes its own World Series, Hall of Fame and coordinates 27 teams.

Image Courtesy of Twitter

Did you know that the chances of a fan being struck by a baseball are 300,000 to 1?

Image Courtesy of j4p4n

Did you know that the "T206 Honus Wagner" baseball card was sold in April 2011 for US$2.8 million making it the most expensive and valuable baseball card in history?

Did you know that during the "Battle of the Bulge", (1944 - 1945), American soldiers used their baseball knowledge to ascertain whether other soldiers were truly Americans or German spies in American uniforms?

Did you know that in baseball the term, "can of corn", refers to a high, fly ball that's very easy to catch?

Image Courtesy of SD Dirk

Did you know that the world's largest baseball bat, weighing 68,000 pounds (30,844 kg) and measuring 120 feet high (3658 cm), can be found outside The Louisville Slugger Museum & Factory in Kentucky, USA.

Image Courtesy of Derek.cashman

Did you know that Babe Ruth, one of the greatest baseball stars of all time, was born George Herman Ruth, played 2503 games and achieved a lifetime batting average of .342?

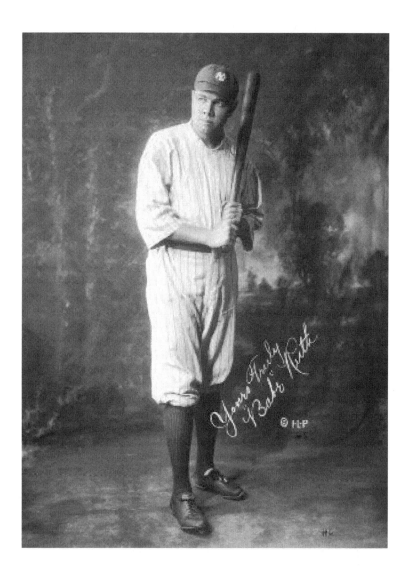

Did you know that baseball "Hall of Famer" James Hoyt
Wilhelm, (nicknamed Old Sarge), hit a home run on his very first
bat in the majors? Despite a career lasting more than 21 years and
going in to bat a total of 432 times, he never managed another
home run.

Did you know that many experts believe Moses Fleetwood Walker was the first African American to have played Major League Baseball, (1884)?

Did you know that on 31st July, 1935, nightclub singer Kitty Burke became the first and only female to ever bat in a Major League Baseball game, (the Cincinnati Reds and the St. Louis Cardinals)?

Image Courtesy of www.todayifoundout.com - Fair Use

Did you know that since its opening in 1912, Fenway Park, (home to the Boston Red Sox MLB team), is the oldest baseball stadium still in use?

Image Courtesy of Jared Vincent

Did you know that in 1996, actor Charlie Sheen spent US$6,500 on 2,615 seats at a California Angels game in the hope that he would be far more likely to catch a home run ball? Unfortunately there were no home runs that day!

Image Courtesy of N0 Photoshop

Did you know that Stan Musial, first baseman in MLB, spent his whole career of 22 years with the St. Louis Cardinals, retiring in 1963 with 3,630 hits? Amazingly, 1,815 hits were at home and 1,815 hits were on the road. What are the odds?

Did you know that in 1963, San Francisco Giants pitcher Gaylord Perry was reported to have said, "They'll put a man on the moon before I hit a home run"? Gaylord managed to hit his first and only home run on 20/7/1969, approximately 20 minutes after Neil Armstrong walked on the moon.

Image Courtesy of twm1340

Did you know that in 1920, Hall of Famer Edd Roush fell asleep on a seat in the outfield during a game? Unable to wake him up, umpires ejected him for delaying the game.

Did you know that in May 1902, William "Dummy" Hoy of the Cincinnati Reds batted against pitcher Luther Haden "Dummy" Taylor of the New York Giants? It was the first time that two deaf players had faced each other in Major League Baseball.

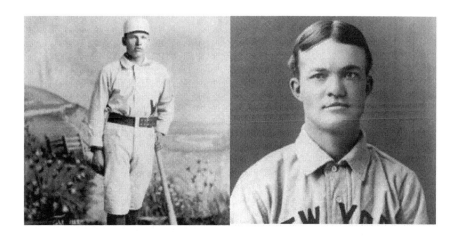

William Hoy & Luther Taylor

Did you know that after his brief career in MLB had ended, Glen Gorbous set an astonishing world record during an exhibition while he was playing for the Omaha Cardinals? On August 1st, 1957, he threw a baseball 445 feet 10 inches, (135.89 meters), from the far right field corner of the stadium to the far left hand corner.

Image Courtesy of John E. Ducey

Did you know that Barry Bonds is currently the only member of the 500–500 club? This means he has hit at least 500 home runs and stolen 500 bases.

Image Courtesy of Kevin Rushforth

Did you know that to date, Tony Cloninger is the only pitcher to have hit 2 grand slams in the same game, (Milwaukee Braves against San Francisco Giants on 3rd July 1966)?

Image Courtesy of www.ogdenonpolitics.com

Did you know that businessman and principal owner of MLB's New York Yankees, George Steinbrenner, once explored the possibility of banning any fan with facial hair entering the Yankees stadium until his legal team persuaded him otherwise?

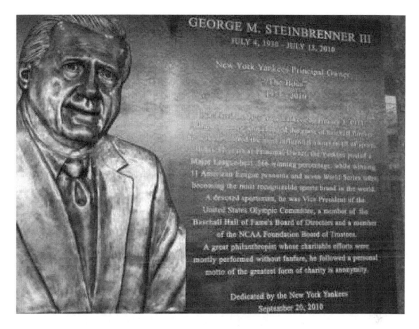

Image Courtesy of Espino Family

Did you know that third baseman "Hall of Famer" Eddie Mathews made history in 1954 when he became the first sportsman to appear on the front cover of the first-ever issue of Sports Illustrated magazine?

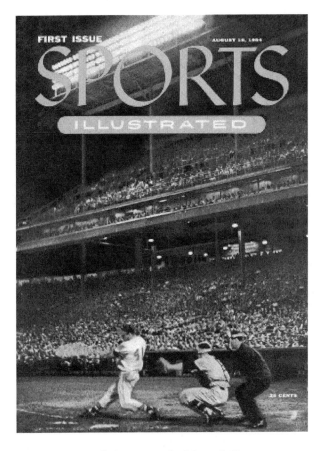

Fair Use: http://photographyblog.dallasnews.com

Did you know that Don Baylor became the first player in Major League Baseball history to play in 3 consecutive World Series for 3 different teams namely the Boston Red Sox - 1986, the Minnesota Twins - 1987 and the Oakland A's - 1988?

Image Courtesy of J. Elden Bailey

Did you know that in 1965, the average annual minimum wage was approximately US$6,000? Today the minimum annual salary is more than US$400,000 and growing!

Image Courtesy of DonkeyHotey

Did you know that since the first official World Series began in 1903, it has only been cancelled twice? The 1904 series was scrapped because the president of the New York Giants, John T. Brush, refused to let his team play the Boston Americans who he considered too inferior! In 1994, it was cancelled due to a players' strike.

John T Brush

That's about it for the baseball trivia for now. I'd like to finish this publication with TEN "True or False" questions based on what you've just read. It should help you to really cement the information and to test your memory recall!

....

....

DON'T FORGET TO KEEP YOUR SCORE: THERE'S 1 POINT FOR EACH OF THE FIRST 9 QUESTIONS AND 5 POINTS FOR THE BONUS QUESTION GIVING A TOTAL OF 14 POINTS ....

1.

TRUE or FALSE: Each baseball game has 12,386,344 possible plays.

TRUE.

2.

TRUE or FALSE: Jon Erich Rauch (pitcher) is the tallest player in MLB history.

TRUE

3.

TRUE or FALSE: A regulation baseball has 108 stitches.

TRUE

4.

TRUE or FALSE: Robert Redford was accepted at the University of Cincinnati on a baseball scholarship.

FALSE

Robert Redford was accepted at the University of **COLORADO** on a baseball scholarship.

5.

TRUE or FALSE: Michael Jack Schmidt was the first player in baseball to earn a salary of US$50,000.

FALSE

Michael Jack Schmidt was the first player in baseball to earn a salary of **US$500,000**.

6.

TRUE or FALSE: Cal Hubbard is the only person you will find in both the Pro-Basketball Hall of Fame & the Baseball Hall of Fame.

FALSE

Cal Hubbard is the only person you will find in both the Pro-**FOOTBALL** Hall of Fame & the Baseball Hall of Fame.

7.

TRUE or FALSE: The chances of a fan being struck by a baseball are 300,000 to 1.

TRUE

8.

TRUE or FALSE: Hall of Famer Edd Roush fell asleep on a seat in the outfield during a game.

TRUE

9.

TRUE or FALSE: Barry Bonds is currently the only member of the 500–500 club.

TRUE

10.

BONUS ROUND WORTH 5 POINTS

TRUE or FALSE: Don Johnson became the first player in Major League Baseball history to play in 3 consecutive World Series for 3 different teams.

FALSE

Don **BAYLOR** became the first player in Major League Baseball history to play in 3 consecutive World Series for 3 different teams.

Congratulations, you made it to the end!

I sincerely hope you enjoyed my little MBL project and that you learnt a thing or two. I certainly did when I was doing the research.

ADD UP YOUR SCORE NOW.

1 point for each of the first 9 correct answers plus 5 points for the bonus round giving a grand total of 14 points.

If you genuinely achieved 14 points then you are indeed an

"MBL MASTER".

8 to 13 points proves you are an **"MBL LEGEND"**.

4 to 7 points shows you are an **"MBL ENTHUSIAST"**.

0 to 3 points shows you are an **"MBL ADMIRER"**.

NICE WORK!

Matt.

Thank you once again for choosing this publication. If you enjoyed it then please let me know using the Customer Review Section through Amazon.

If you would like to read more of my work then simply type in my name using the Amazon Search Box and hopefully you'll find something else that "takes your fancy" or go directly to my website printed below.

Until we meet again,

Matthew Harper

www.matthewharper.info

Image Courtesy of laobc

Made in the USA
San Bernardino, CA
05 April 2017